WHEN, WHERE, WHAT
QUIZZES

D1420338

First published in 2002 by Miles Kelly Publishing Ltd,
Bardfield Centre, Great Bardfield, Essex, CM7 4SL

Copyright © Miles Kelly Publishing Ltd 2002

This edition printed 2002

ISBN 1-84236-136-8

2 4 6 8 10 9 7 5 3

Project Manager: Ian Paulyn
Assistant: Lisa Clayden
Design: Clare Sleven

Contact us by email: info@mileskelly.net
Website: www.mileskelly.net

Printed in India

WHEN, WHERE, WHAT
QUIZZES

by
Christopher Rigby

Miles Kelly
PUBLISHING

About the Author

Born in Blackburn, Lancashire in 1960, Christopher Rigby has been compiling and presenting pub quizzes for the past 15 years. When he is not adding to his material for quizzes, Christopher works in the car industry. He is married to Clare – they have two teenage daughters, Hollie and Ashley and share their home with two demented dogs called Vespa and Bailey. A keen Manchester United fan Christopher lists his heroes as George Best and Homer Simpson.

WHERE, WHEN & WHAT EXPLAINED

This quiz book comprises 90 quizzes on a variety of themes. The object of each quiz is to attempt to identify the answer as quickly as possible with the help of five clues, which get gradually easier as the points value
is reduced.

Below is an example:

NAME THE YEAR

5 POINT CLUE Phil Taylor won his 9th World Darts Championship and the Baltimore Ravens won their first ever Superbowl.

4 POINT CLUE Ronald Reagan celebrated his 90th birthday and Clara Furse became the first ever female boss of the Stock Exchange.

3 POINT CLUE This year saw the 100th anniversary of the death of Queen Victoria and pop group Coldplay won three Brit Awards including Best Group.

2 POINT CLUE The world of entertainment mourned the deaths of Michael Williams and Sir Harry Secombe.

1 POINT CLUE In *EastEnders* Lisa Shaw shot Phil Mitchell and at the Oscars *Gladiator* was voted Best Film.

Answer 2001

NAME THE COUNTRY

5 POINT CLUE This country covers an area of 312,678 square kilometres (120,725 square miles) and approximately 95% of its population adhere to the Roman Catholic religion. Its national day falls on May 3rd.

4 POINT CLUE In 1981 martial law was declared in this country but in 1992 the state monopoly of radio and television was ended. The River Oder flows through the western boundaries of this country.

3 POINT CLUE Cities in this country include Katowice and Gdansk. To the north lies the Baltic Sea and to the south lies the Czech Republic.

2 POINT CLUE The 1990 Nobel Peace Prize winner, a former electrician, was elected President of this country and in September 1939 this country was invaded by Germany.

1 POINT CLUE Its capital city is Warsaw and Pope John Paul II hails from this country.

ANSWER
POLAND

NAME THE YEAR

5 POINT CLUE In this year Carlo Ripa de Meano, the European Commissioner for the Environment, took Britain to court over its polluted beaches. Also in this year Bruce Kent retired as the Chairman of the CND and Norman Fowler quit the post of Employment Secretary.

4 POINT CLUE On June 24th of this year the first Anglican female priests were ordained in Belfast. Gordon Jackson, star of many TV dramas including *Upstairs, Downstairs*, died on January 14th of this year.

3 POINT CLUE Annie Lennox was voted Best Female Singer at the Brit Awards and Sinead O'Connor topped the singles charts with the haunting melody 'Nothing Compares 2 U'.

2 POINT CLUE In January of this year boxer Terry Marsh was acquitted of the attempted murder of promoter Frank Warren. In August of this year £5 coins were circulated throughout Britain for the first time.

1 POINT CLUE This year saw the release of Nelson Mandela from prison and the release of a flood of tears from Paul Gascoigne in the World Cup semi-finals.

ANSWER
1990

NAME THE POP GROUP

5 POINT CLUE This pop group was formed in 1982 under the name of the Vortex Motion, but took a new name from a line in the Scritti Pollitti song, 'Getting, Having And Holding'.

4 POINT CLUE They had to wait until 1987 for their first hit single and the following year they were voted Best British Newcomers at the Brit Awards.

3 POINT CLUE They had three No. 1 singles in the 20th century and a No. 1 album entitled 'Popped In Souled Out'.

2 POINT CLUE The real name of their lead singer is Mark McLoughlin and their first hit single was entitled 'Wishing I Was Lucky'.

1 POINT CLUE In 1994 they spent 15 weeks at No. 1 with a song which featured in the film *Four Weddings And A Funeral*.

ANSWER
WET, WET, WET

NAME THE TV PROGRAMME

5 POINT CLUE This TV programme was first shown on British television in 1979 and the star of the show went on to become one of Hollywood's biggest box office film stars.

4 POINT CLUE It was set in the American town of Boulder and the supporting cast included the actor Ralph James and the actress Elizabeth Kerr.

3 POINT CLUE Characters in the show included Mr Bickley and an eccentric prophet named Exidor.

2 POINT CLUE The female lead role was played by Pam Dawber and the lead male character was often heard shouting 'Shazbat' when he was annoyed.

1 POINT CLUE In this show Robin Williams played an alien who landed on Earth in a giant egg with a mission to study earthlings.

ANSWER
MORK & MINDY

NAME THE SONG

5 POINT CLUE This song was a hit on four separate occasions in the 20th century including an instrumental version. It was originally a hit in 1977.

4 POINT CLUE It sold 980,000 copies in the UK when topping the charts in 1977 for a female singer and its original title was 'It's Only Your Lover Returning'.

3 POINT CLUE It was covered in 1978 by the Shadows, in 1992 by Sinead O'Connor and in 1996 by both Madonna and Mike Flowers Pop.

2 POINT CLUE The title of the song contains the name of a country and the artist who topped the charts with this song starred in the TV series *Rock Follies*.

1 POINT CLUE It was written by Tim Rice and Andrew Lloyd Webber for the stage musical *Evita*.

ANSWER
'DON'T CRY FOR ME, ARGENTINA'.

NAME THE COUNTRY

5 POINT CLUE This small country only covers 2,585 square kilometres (998 square miles) and has a population of less than 1 million. Its national day falls on 23rd June and its flag comprises of three horizontal bands of red, white and blue.

4 POINT CLUE It was established as an independent state under the sovereignty of the King of the Netherlands by the Congress of Vienna in 1815.

3 POINT CLUE Its capital city, with a population of approximately 80,000, is a dismantled fortress and in 1867 the Treaty of London declared this country a neutral territory.

2 POINT CLUE The official language of this country is Letzeburgesch but most of its citizens speak French and German.

1 POINT CLUE It is classed as a Grand Duchy and forms boundaries with Germany, Belgium and France.

NAME THE FILM

5 POINT CLUE This film, 145 minutes long, was released in 1968 and featured the child actors, Adrian Hall and Heather Ripley, who played a brother and sister called Jeremy and Jemima.

4 POINT CLUE The cast of the film included Lionel Jeffries, Gert Frobe, Benny Hill, Max Wall, Barbara Windsor and James Robertson Justice.

3 POINT CLUE Songs that featured in the film include 'Hushaby Mountain', 'Lovely Lonely Man', 'Toot Sweet' and 'Chu Chi Face'.

2 POINT CLUE The lead character in the film was an eccentric inventor called Caractacus Potts and the screenplay was written by Roald Dahl and based on a novel by Ian Fleming.

1 POINT CLUE The title of this film took its name from the name of a flying car which was operated by Dick Van Dyke.

ANSWER
CHITTY CHITTY BANG BANG

NAME THE FOOTBALL TEAM

5 POINT CLUE This football team was founded in 1882, and their first recorded match in 1883 resulted in an 8–1 defeat inflicted on them by a team called Latymer. In 1892 they joined the Southern League and finished the season in 3rd place.

4 POINT CLUE They first entered into the FA Cup in 1895 and were eventually knocked out by West Herts, losing 3–2. They joined the Football League in 1908 and finished 2nd in their first season.

3 POINT CLUE In 1901 whilst still a non league team they famously won the FA Cup beating Sheffield United 3–1 in the final. Sixty years later they won the League and FA Cup double.

2 POINT CLUE Famous players to have graced this team's shirt include Jimmy Greaves, Alan Mullery, Pat Jennings, Gary Lineker and Danny Blanchflower.

1 POINT CLUE In 2001 former player Glen Hoddle replaced George Graham as the manager of this club, who play their home matches at White Hart Lane.

ANSWER
TOTTENHAM HOTSPUR

NAME THE YEAR

5 POINT CLUE This year saw the foundation of the Save the Seals Fund and in the same year Samuel Beckett won the Nobel Prize for Literature.

4 POINT CLUE In March of this year John Lennon and Yoko Ono had their infamous 'Bed in for peace' demonstration in an Amsterdam hotel. Also in this year Lennon's fellow Beatle Paul McCartney married Linda Eastman.

3 POINT CLUE A certain Margaret Thatcher was appointed Shadow Spokesman for Education and El Salvador went to war with Honduras over a football match.

2 POINT CLUE In the world of sport Jackie Stewart won the Italian Grand Prix, a teenage Peter Shilton played in the FA Cup Final and Rocky Marciano perished in a plane crash.

1 POINT CLUE This was the year when Neil Armstrong became the first man to set foot on the moon.

ANSWER
1969

NAME THE SPORT

5 POINT CLUE This sport originated from a German game called Heidenwerfen.

4 POINT CLUE National champions of years gone by include Ray Tobias, Arnold Thornleigh and Larry Sedgeman.

3 POINT CLUE It was exported to the USA in the 17th century but was banned in some states from 1840. A subtle change in the rules was instigated to overcome this ban and it is now amongst the most popular pastimes in the USA.

2 POINT CLUE Its original name Heidenwerfen, when translated into English literally means 'knock down pagans'.

1 POINT CLUE The maximum score in a single game is 300, which consists of 12 strikes.

ANSWER
TEN-PIN BOWLING

NAME THE COUNTRY

5 POINT CLUE This country has an approximate population of 4.5 million and is 1,752 kilometres (1089 miles) in length but is only 430 kilometres (267 miles) at its widest point.

4 POINT CLUE It is a member of NATO and its main exports include crude oil and fish products. Major towns in the country include Trondheim and Bergen.

3 POINT CLUE The painter Edvard Munch hailed from this country and it is nicknamed 'The land of the midnight sun'.

2 POINT CLUE The krone is the currency unit of this country and its flag is red with a white bordered blue cross.

1 POINT CLUE This country forms a border with Sweden and its capital city is Oslo.

ANSWER
NORWAY

NAME THE YEAR

5 POINT CLUE In this year the Reserve Bank of Australia issued the world's first plastic bank note and 80 spectators were killed in a stampede at a football stadium in Katmandu.

4 POINT CLUE Kahyasi won the Epsom Derby in this year and films of the year included *Big* starring Tom Hanks and *Coming To America* starring Eddie Murphy.

3 POINT CLUE Dog licences were abolished in Britain and the controversial novel *The Satanic Verses* went on sale in British bookshops.

2 POINT CLUE Cliff Richard topped the Christmas charts with the song 'Mistletoe and Wine' and 33 people died in a train crash at Clapham Junction.

I POINT CLUE 243 people died in the Lockerbie air crash and in this year Seoul hosted the Summer Olympic games.

ANSWER
1988

NAME THE POP GROUP

5 POINT CLUE This pop group was formed in the winter of 1993 and made their TV debut on *The Late, Late Show* dancing to a backing track. Their first single, a cover version of 'Working My Way Back To You', failed to chart.

4 POINT CLUE At the 1996 Brit Awards they won gongs for Best Album, Best Single and Best International Group.

3 POINT CLUE Their first UK hit single was a cover version of the Osmonds' hit 'Love Me For A Reason' and they went on to perform the theme music for the film *Bean* starring Rowan Atkinson.

2 POINT CLUE One of the group's members has twin sisters in the group Bewitched, another appeared in *Celebrity Big Brother* and the most famous member went on to manage the boy band Westlife.

1 POINT CLUE They topped the charts with the song 'No Matter What' and their lead singer Ronan Keating has enjoyed several solo No. 1 hits including 'Life Is A Rollercoaster'.

ANSWER
BOYZONE

NAME THE TV PROGRAMME

5 POINT CLUE This TV programme first appeared on British TV in 1990. It won several BAFTAs including Best Comedy Series and also won a 1992 Emmy Award for Best International Popular Arts.

4 POINT CLUE Neil Kinnock and Ken Livingstone have both made appearances on this show.

3 POINT CLUE Characters in the show include Gus Hedges, George Dent and Damien Day who were all employees of Sir Royston Merchant.

2 POINT CLUE The actor Neil Pearson played Dave Charnley in the show, the title of which contains the name of an equine creature.

1 POINT CLUE This Channel 4 comedy featured the activities of the Globe Link TV news team.

ANSWER
DROP THE DEAD DONKEY

NAME THE SONG

5 POINT CLUE This song topped the UK singles charts for three weeks and was written by Albert Hammond and Carole Bayer-Sager. It topped the charts in 1977 on the Chrysalis record label.

4 POINT CLUE The singer of the song was born in the town of Shoreham, Sussex in 1948 and was discovered and managed by the sixties star Adam Faith.

3 POINT CLUE In 1998 this song reached No. 5 in the UK singles charts when it was covered by the actor Will Mellor.

2 POINT CLUE This song contained the line 'Telephone can't take the place of your smile'.

1 POINT CLUE This song was the only No. 1 hit for Leo Sayer.

ANSWER
'WHEN I NEED YOU.'

QUIZ SIX

5 POINT CLUE This city was the original burial place of St Swithun and the Saint Cross Hospital lies one mile south of this city.

4 POINT CLUE This city also boasts a 13th-century building called the Great Hall which was built during the reign of Henry III and houses the Arthurian Round Table.

3 POINT CLUE This city stands on the River Itchen and 20th-century excavations uncovered a Roman town and an Anglo-Saxon Cathedral, known as the Old Minster.

2 POINT CLUE This city was the capital of England before London.

1 POINT CLUE The world's longest gothic cathedral can be found in this city, which shares its name with a type of rifle.

ANSWER
WINCHESTER

NAME THE FILM

....

5 POINT CLUE This film based on a true story was adapted from a book by Robin Moore. A sequel followed in 1975.

4 POINT CLUE It won an Academy Award for Best Film, and one of the cast went on to star as Chief Brody in the film *Jaws*.

3 POINT CLUE It was made in 1971 and was directed by William Friedkin and featured a memorable car chase involving an elevated railway.

2 POINT CLUE The 1971 original was set in New York, whilst the majority of the action in the 1975 sequel was set in Marseilles.

1 POINT CLUE Gene Hackman won much critical acclaim for his portrayal of hard-bitten cop Popeye Doyle in this film.

NAME THE CREATURE

5 POINT CLUE It is estimated that this creature has lived on our planet for around 140 million years, and some species have up to 110 teeth.

4 POINT CLUE It is indigenous in Asia, Australia, Africa, North and South America and it lays hard-shelled eggs.

3 POINT CLUE Species of this animal include the Orinoco, Morelet's, Cuban, African dwarf, Philippine, mugger and gharial.

2 POINT CLUE Its life span can range from 10 years to 70 years depending on the species, some of which can grow to over 20 feet in length. In 1972 Elton John had a Top 10 hit record singing about one of these fearsome creatures.

1 POINT CLUE In the film and book *Peter Pan* this animal swallowed an alarm clock and one of Captain Hook's hands.

ANSWER
CROCODILE

NAME THE YEAR

5 POINT CLUE In this year Upper Volta changed its name to Burkina Faso and Len Murray retired as the General Secretary of the TUC.

4 POINT CLUE Famous people who died this year included Tommy Cooper, Diana Dors, Yuri Andropov, John Betjeman and James Mason.

3 POINT CLUE The magazine *Titbits* folded in this year and York Minster was badly damaged by a fire.

2 POINT CLUE WPC Yvonne Fletcher was shot dead and British civil servant Clive Ponting was charged under the Official Secrets Act after admitting to leaking documents relating to the Falklands War.

1 POINT CLUE Carl Lewis won four gold medals and the title of a famous novel by George Orwell should lead you to this year.

ANSWER
1984

NAME THE MONTH

5 POINT CLUE The Arab-Israeli War of 1973 began in this month and the Nottingham Goose Fair is held in this month.

4 POINT CLUE The Alderburgh Benjamin Britten music festival is held in this month, and a 1981 album by U2 shares its title with this month.

3 POINT CLUE If you were born in this month your star sign would be either Libra or Scorpio.

2 POINT CLUE The name of this month literally means 'eighth month'.

1 POINT CLUE Halloween falls in this month.

ANSWER
OCTOBER

NAME THE COUNTRY

5 POINT CLUE The area of this country is estimated at 20,769 square kilometres (8,019 square miles) and its population is between 5 and 6 million. The highest mountain in this country is called Mount Meron.

4 POINT CLUE There are a total of seven universities in this country and one of its chief ports is called Ashdod.

3 POINT CLUE Its chief airport is called the Ben Gurion airport and its official languages are Hebrew and Arabic.

2 POINT CLUE It is bordered by Lebanon on the north, Syria on the north-east and Jordan on the west. The principal river in this country is the River Jordan which flows through the Hula Valley.

1 POINT CLUE The cities of Jerusalem and Tel Aviv can be found in this country.

ANSWER
ISRAEL

NAME THE YEAR

5 POINT CLUE In this year the new £5 note was issued in the UK featuring Britannia without her helmet. Also in this year the first British-made oral contraceptive became available on prescription.

4 POINT CLUE Valentina Tereshkova became the first woman in space and Harold Wilson defeated George Brown in the battle for the Labour leadership.

3 POINT CLUE George Michael and Andrew Ridgeley were both born in this year and the last 27 prisoners vacated the notorious Alcatraz Prison when it closed on 21st March.

2 POINT CLUE John Profumo resigned and the Beatles had their first UK Top 10 hit with the song 'Please, Please Me'.

1 POINT CLUE This year witnessed the Great Train Robbery and the assassination of John F Kennedy.

ANSWER
1963

NAME THE POP GROUP

5 POINT CLUE This pop group was formed in 1977 and the following year embarked on a 16 date UK tour supporting Talking Heads.

4 POINT CLUE The band's original line-up was John, Hal, Pick, Mark and Alan.

3 POINT CLUE Hit albums for the group include *Alchemy*, *Communique*, *Making Movies* and *Love Over Gold*.

2 POINT CLUE The group's leader wrote the music for the film *Local Hero* and in 1979 they had their first hit single with the song 'Sultans Of Swing'.

I POINT CLUE Their album *Brothers In Arms* became one of the best-selling CDs and featured the song 'Money For Nothing', with a joint vocal performance from Mark Knopfler and Sting.

ANSWER
DIRE STRAITS

NAME THE TV PROGRAMME

5 POINT CLUE This mystery TV programme was created by Roy Clarke and was developed from a 1973 Comedy Playhouse piece entitled *Of Funerals And Fish*.

4 POINT CLUE The supporting cast over the years has featured many familiar faces including Gordon Kaye, Stephen Lewis, Jean Ferguson and Jean Alexander.

3 POINT CLUE It has been described by a TV critic as 'Just William with pension books', and despite the criticism it has become Britain's longest-running sitcom.

2 POINT CLUE Characters in the show have included Seymour Utterthwaite and café proprietors Ivy and Sid, and it is set in a village called Holmfirth.

1 POINT CLUE This sitcom featured the misadventures of Compo, Foggy and Cleggy, whose antics were always met by stony disapproval from Nora Batty.

ANSWER
LAST OF THE SUMMER WINE

NAME THE NOVEL

5 POINT CLUE The author of this novel began writing it in July 1830 and it was completed in January 1831. It was first translated into English in July 1833.

4 POINT CLUE It was set in the year of 1482 and has been filmed many times including a 1996 animated Disney production which featured the voices of Kevin Kline and Demi Moore.

3 POINT CLUE The hero of this novel is called Captain Phoebus and the villain is called Archdeacon Frollo.

2 POINT CLUE This novel is set in the city of Paris and the many stars who have appeared in filmed versions include Gina Lollobrigida, Anthony Quinn, Lon Chaney and Charles Laughton.

1 POINT CLUE Victor Hugo penned this novel which featured a campanologist called Quasimodo.

ANSWER
THE HUNCHBACK OF NOTRE DAME

NAME THE COUNTRY

5 POINT CLUE This country has a total area of 449,966 kilometres (173,732 square miles) and over 95% of the population adhere to the state religion of Lutheran Protestant.

4 POINT CLUE The basis of its language was formed by Olaus Petri. Notable writers from this country include Almquist and Lagerlof, the latter of whom won the Nobel Prize for Literature in 1909.

3 POINT CLUE The country's flag features a yellow cross on a blue background and in September 1973 Carl XVI Gustav was crowned king.

2 POINT CLUE Major cities in this country include Malmo and Uppsala, and it occupies the eastern area of the Scandinavian Peninsula.

1 POINT CLUE Tennis star Bjorn Borg and the pop group Abba both hail from this country.

ANSWER
SWEDEN

NAME THE FILM

5 POINT CLUE This film was directed by Barry Sonnenfield in 1997. It cost $90 million to make but grossed over $500 million world-wide.

4 POINT CLUE The film earned Oscars for Rick Baker and David Leroy Anderson in the Best Makeup category.

3 POINT CLUE The supporting cast included Siobhan Fallon, Rip Torn and Tony Shalhoub and a cat called Orion.

2 POINT CLUE The theme song for the film was a huge rap hit and was performed by one of the film's leading stars. The film ended with one of the main characters waking up from an alleged 30-year coma.

1 POINT CLUE This film co-starred Tommy Lee Jones & Will Smith as alien hunters.

ANSWER
MEN IN BLACK

NAME THE CARTOON CHARACTER

5 POINT CLUE This cartoon character first appeared on American TV in 1958 and on British TV two years later. The voice of this character was provided by Daws Butler.

4 POINT CLUE In 1973 it was the subject of Hanna Barbera's first feature-length cartoon film, and it began life as a segment of the *Huckleberry Hound Show*.

3 POINT CLUE He wore a pork pie hat and his favourite food was blueberry pie which he often stole from unsuspecting tourists.

2 POINT CLUE His adversary was called John Smith, who was the ranger of Jellystone National Park.

I POINT CLUE He claimed that he was 'Smarter than the average bear' and was partnered by his best buddy Boo Boo the bear.

ANSWER
YOGI BEAR

NAME THE YEAR

5 POINT CLUE In this year Jerry Rawlings became the leader of Ghana, the Queen opened the Nat West Tower and France abolished the death penalty.

4 POINT CLUE British garages began selling petrol by the litre, and Debbie Harry left Blondie in an attempt to forge a solo career.

3 POINT CLUE In the world of sport Torvill & Dean won their first European title and a wonder goal from Ricardo Villa won the FA Cup for Tottenham Hotspur.

2 POINT CLUE The Gang of Four founded the SDP in this year which also saw the death of Bill Haley and the arrest of Peter Sutcliffe.

1 POINT CLUE There were failed assassination attempts on Ronald Reagan and the Pope but a successful one on Anwar Sadat.

NAME THE FICTIONAL CHARACTER

5 POINT CLUE This fictional character has appeared in several films over the years, the first of which came in 1945. Three sequels followed in the 1940s and an updated version was filmed in 1990.

4 POINT CLUE This character originated from a comic strip created by Chester Gould.

3 POINT CLUE His adversaries have included such weird and wonderful names as Cueball, Splitface and Gruesome.

2 POINT CLUE Stars who have appeared in the films over the years include Boris Karloff, Al Pacino, Lex Barker, Dustin Hoffman, Dick Van Dyke and Madonna.

I POINT CLUE This fictional detective was played on film in 1990 by Warren Beatty.

ANSWER
DICK TRACY

NAME THE CITY

5 POINT CLUE This city first appeared on early European maps over 1,000 years ago. Until the 12th century it was a fishing village and was granted its first civil charter in 1254.

4 POINT CLUE In 1443 it was chosen as its country's capital city by Christopher III. Today this city is a major sea port and commercial centre for textiles, sugar refineries and distilling.

3 POINT CLUE Between 1940 and 1945 it was occupied by German troops and in 1801 this city gave its name to a major naval battle.

2 POINT CLUE It shares its name with the Duke of Wellington's horse and it can be found on an island called Zealand.

1 POINT CLUE You could visit the Tivoli gardens in this city, the capital city of Denmark.

ANSWER
COPENHAGEN

NAME THE YEAR

5 POINT CLUE The Pompidou Centre opened its doors this year in Paris and the Piccadilly Line on London's underground was extended to Heathrow Airport.

4 POINT CLUE Amnesty International won the Nobel Peace Prize, and Kerry Packer coaxed 35 of the world's best cricketers to join his cricket circus.

3 POINT CLUE Glen Matlock was sacked from the Sex Pistols after he admitted that he liked the Beatles, and the movie world was in mourning over the death of Charlie Chaplin.

2 POINT CLUE Jimmy Carter was inaugurated as American president and Red Rum romped to his third Grand National victory.

I POINT CLUE Street parties abounded around Britain to celebrate the Queen's Silver Jubilee and the King of Rock and Roll, Elvis Presley, died.

ANSWER
1977

NAME THE POP GROUP

5 POINT CLUE This pop group was formed in 1965 from the remnants of various other bands which included Rick and the Ravens and the Psyched Rangers.

4 POINT CLUE In 1969 the group appeared in a film about themselves entitled *Feast Of Friends*. The previous year they released their debut album, which was called *Waiting For The Sun*.

3 POINT CLUE They took their name from a book by Aldous Huxley and their first Top 20 UK hit single came in 1968 and was called 'Hello I Love You'.

2 POINT CLUE In 1991 Oliver Stone directed a film about this group which starred Val Kilmer as the lead singer.

I POINT CLUE In July of 1971 the lead singer Jim Morrison was found dead in a bath tub in Paris and was buried six days later in the Pere Lachaise Cemetery.

ANSWER
THE DOORS

NAME THE TV PROGRAMME

5 POINT CLUE This TV programme debuted in the USA in 1973, and featured an organisation called the Office of Strategic Investigations.

4 POINT CLUE The last in the series was made in 1978, however it was revived in 1987 for two TV films. In this adventure series Alan Oppenheimer played Dr Rudy Wells.

3 POINT CLUE It was based on a Martin Caidin novel called *Cyborg* and spawned a spin-off in 1976, which featured the character of Jamie Summers.

2 POINT CLUE Richard Anderson as Oscar Goldman opened each episode with the words 'Gentlemen, we have the technology, we have the capability, we can rebuild him'.

1 POINT CLUE Lee Majors played Colonel Steve Austin in this TV series.

ANSWER
THE SIX MILLION DOLLAR MAN

NAME THE NOVEL

5 POINT CLUE This novel, which took seven years to complete, was started in 1928. The writer was born in Atlanta and died there in tragic circumstances following a car crash in 1949.

4 POINT CLUE The novel sold over 10 million copies world-wide and won a Pulitzer Prize. In the very first line of the novel we are introduced to the characters of the Tarleton twins.

3 POINT CLUE Other characters include Cade Clavert and Ashley Wilkes and it is set against the American Civil War.

2 POINT CLUE It is the only novel by Margaret Mitchell and a lavish film production was made in 1939 and ended with the words 'After all tomorrow is another day'.

1 POINT CLUE The chief character in the novel is called Scarlett O'Hara, who was played on film by Vivien Leigh.

ANSWER
GONE WITH THE WIND

NAME THE COUNTRY

5 POINT CLUE This country has a population slightly below that of the UK and in 1987 Lieutenant Colonel Mengistu became the president.

4 POINT CLUE There are 15 major ethnic groups that are native to this country, speaking a total of 70 different languages, of which the most widely used is Amharic.

3 POINT CLUE It forms boundaries with several countries two of which are Sudan and Somalia.

2 POINT CLUE It was formerly called Abyssinia and the athlete nicknamed 'Yifter the Shifter' won two Olympic gold medals representing this country.

1 POINT CLUE The capital city of this African country is Addis Ababa.

ANSWER
ETHIOPIA

NAME THE FILM

5 POINT CLUE This Oscar-winning film was adapted from an novel by Margaret Landon, and the lead actress's singing voice was dubbed by Mami Nixon.

4 POINT CLUE It was originally a stage show and was transferred to the big screen in 1956. Forty-three years later an animated version was released featuring the voices of Miranda Richardson and Sean Smith.

3 POINT CLUE Songs from the film include 'I Whistle A Happy Tune', 'Hello Young Lovers', 'Something Wonderful' and 'Getting To Know You'.

2 POINT CLUE This film was set in a country that is now called Thailand and Oscar Hammerstein wrote the music for the film.

I POINT CLUE This film was a musical remake of *Anna and the King of Siam* and starred Yul Brynner in the role of the king.

ANSWER
THE KING AND I

NAME THE CITY

5 POINT CLUE This city has a population of approximately 1 million, and its major manufacturing industries include textiles and chocolate.

4 POINT CLUE This city is home to 'The Shrine of Magic' which reputedly contains the fossilised bones of the Three Wise Men.

3 POINT CLUE This city contains a famous gothic cathedral which has twin spires each of which is 157 metres (515 feet) high. The building of this cathedral commenced in 1248 and was not completed until 1880.

2 POINT CLUE This city can be found in the country of Germany and it stands on the River Rhine.

1 POINT CLUE This city gave its name to a famous perfumed liquid.

ANSWER
COLOGNE

NAME THE YEAR

5 POINT CLUE In this year India carried out its first ever nuclear bomb test, and Sir Stanley Rous retired as President of FIFA.

4 POINT CLUE A 19-year-old Chris Evert became Wimbledon Champion and Patty Hearst was kidnapped.

3 POINT CLUE Kevin Keegan scored two goals in the FA Cup Final and Swedish popsters Abba won the Eurovision Song Contest.

2 POINT CLUE Rutland was swallowed up by Leicestershire and Nelson Rockefeller was appointed vice president to Gerald Ford.

1 POINT CLUE There was an attempted kidnap of Princess Anne on March 20th of this year, and West Germany beat Holland 2-1 to win football's World Cup.

ANSWER
1974

NAME THE DOG BREED

5 POINT CLUE This breed of dog is thought to have originated in the 16th century and an alternative name for this breed is the Teckel, with the miniature variety called the Zwergteckel.

4 POINT CLUE The standard breed of this dog stands only 21 to 23 centimetres (8 to 9 inches) in height, whilst the miniature breed is even smaller and weighs less than 5 kilograms (11 pounds).

3 POINT CLUE It was originally bred for hunting and it is a cross between a miniature French pointer and a pinscher.

2 POINT CLUE This dog originated in Germany and has a German name which, when translated into English, literally means 'Badger dog'.

1 POINT CLUE This dog's short stumpy legs and relatively long body have resulted in this breed being nicknamed the 'Sausage dog'.

ANSWER
DACHSHUND

NAME THE COUNTRY

5 POINT CLUE This country has a total area of 164,150 square kilometres, (63,378 square miles) and a population approaching 9 million. From 1881 it was a French protectorate until it gained its independence in 1956.

4 POINT CLUE The flag of this country is red with a white disc that contains a red crescent and star.

3 POINT CLUE The national anthem of this country is called 'Himat Al Hima', and the country lies between Algeria and Libya and extends southwards to the Sahara Desert.

2 POINT CLUE Its currency unit is the dinar and the ancient ruins of Carthage are located a few miles away from this country's capital city.

1 POINT CLUE Tunis is the capital city of this country.

ANSWER
TUNISIA

NAME THE YEAR

5 POINT CLUE In this year the island of Iwo Jima, captured by the USA in 1945, returned to Japan. Also in this year the Legoland theme park opened in Denmark.

4 POINT CLUE David Owen, aged 30, became the Government's youngest MP and Alex Smith became Britain's first lung transplant patient.

3 POINT CLUE This year saw the deaths of Enid Blyton, Bud Flanagan and motor-racer Jim Clark. Also in this year the *Queen Elizabeth* Cunard liner was pensioned off.

2 POINT CLUE Jackie Kennedy married Aristotle Onassis, and Robert Kennedy was the victim of an assassin's bullet.

1 POINT CLUE In the world of sport Manchester City won the League Championship, whilst their neighbours Manchester United defeated Benfica to win the European Cup.

ANSWER
1968

NAME THE POP GROUP

5 POINT CLUE The four members of this pop group first played together in 1966 in a group called the 'N Betweens. Their first two albums, entitled *Beginnings* and *Play It Loud* both failed to chart.

4 POINT CLUE In 1970 they signed to the Polydor record label and had their first hit single a year later with a cover version of a Bobby Marchan song.

3 POINT CLUE This group had six No. 1 hits during the 1970s, and their last top 10 hit in 1984 with a song called 'Run, Runaway'.

2 POINT CLUE The lead singer of the band has since taken to playing a teacher in *The Grimleys*, and ironically this group were criticised by the teaching profession for deliberately spelling record titles incorrectly.

1 POINT CLUE Noddy Holder was the lead singer of this glam rock act who had a famous yuletide No. 1 with 'Merry Xmas Everybody'.

NAME THE TV PROGRAMME

5 POINT CLUE This TV programme was set in suburban Bournemouth and won a host of TV awards for its creator David Renwick and the actors who appeared in it.

4 POINT CLUE The main character's job before retiring was as a security guard for Mycroft, Watts & Associates. The show was sold to America in the 90s where it was remade with Bill Cosby in the lead role.

3 POINT CLUE This sitcom featured Angus Deayton and Janine Duvitski as neighbours Patrick and Pippa.

2 POINT CLUE The lead character was killed off when he was knocked down by a car driven by the actress Hannah Gordon.

I POINT CLUE This show featured Richard Wilson who played grumpy Victor Meldrew.

ANSWER
ONE FOOT IN THE GRAVE

NAME THE NOVEL

5 POINT CLUE This novel set in the 1840s was published in 1874, was sold out in just two months and was written by a 33-year-old author.

4 POINT CLUE The opening chapter of this novel introduces the reader to one of the main characters, a farmer by the name of Gabriel Oak.

3 POINT CLUE It is set like the majority of the author's works in Wessex. Other novels attributed to the author include *Under The Greenwood Tree* and *Tess Of The D' Urbervilles*.

2 POINT CLUE The main plot of the novel concerns the female character of Bathsheba Everdene and her three suitors vying for her hand in marriage.

1 POINT CLUE Thomas Hardy wrote this novel. An anagram of this novel's title is MADAME C WORD FROTHING FRED.

ANSWER
FAR FROM THE MADDING CROWD

NAME THE TOWN

5 POINT CLUE This English coastal town boasts one of the largest Bingo clubs in Britain, which is named the Northern Parade Social Club.

4 POINT CLUE During the early 19th century its population was only 500, but the population grew when the railway system was extended to the coast in 1875, and today the population is over 20,000.

3 POINT CLUE It is estimated that tourism brings over £200 million a year to this town and during the month of August tourists swell the population to over 100,000.

2 POINT CLUE This seaside resort is 209 kilometres (130 miles) away from London and the same distance away from Manchester, and Billy Butlin opened his first holiday camp here.

1 POINT CLUE It is found in the county of Lincolnshire and its motto is 'It's So Bracing'.

ANSWER
SKEGNESS

NAME THE FILM

5 POINT CLUE This film was released in 1983 by Paramount Pictures. It was directed by Adrian Lyne and was set in Pittsburgh.

4 POINT CLUE It was a huge box office success but it was savaged by the critics. One critic wrote 'It resembles an extended video for a record album. This film is a ridiculous success'.

3 POINT CLUE The film earned a Best Song Oscar for Giorgio Moroder and that song was performed by Irene Cara.

2 POINT CLUE The cast included Belinda Bauer, Sunny Johnson and Michael Nouri, and the lead role was played by Jennifer Beals.

1 POINT CLUE It tells the story of a female welder who fulfils her aspiration of becoming a ballet dancer.

WHAT IS IT?

5 POINT CLUE Its name derives from the Greek word *Smaragdos* and it is formed by rising magma and metamorphism.

4 POINT CLUE It rates between 7 and 8 on the Moh's hardness scale, and its crystals are usually hexagonal.

3 POINT CLUE It is mined throughout the world with important mines found near Bogota in Columbia and the Habach Valley near Salzburg in Austria.

2 POINT CLUE The song 'Feel The Need In Me' was a hit for a group from Detroit whose full name should lead you to this precious gem that belongs to the beryl group of stones.

1 POINT CLUE The name Smaragdos, when translated into English, literally means 'Green stone'.

NAME THE YEAR

5 POINT CLUE In this year the alleged diary of Jack the Ripper was published and the animal rights organisation LYNX changed its name to Respect For Animals.

4 POINT CLUE The Pope visited Sicily in this year and caused controversy when he denounced the Mafia. Also in this year Lloyd Bentsen was appointed the Secretary Treasurer of the Clinton administration.

3 POINT CLUE The highly controversial drama *The Buddha of Suburbia* was shown on British TV and the Queen became a tax payer.

2 POINT CLUE No. I hits of this year included 'Young At Heart' by the Bluebells and 'Relight My Fire' by Take That, featuring Lulu. The Christmas No. I hit was performed by a pink TV character with yellow dots.

I POINT CLUE Captain Keith Brown made a complete hash of starting the Grand National and this race that never was, was 'won' by a horse called Esha Ness.

ANSWER
1993

NAME THE BIRD

5 POINT CLUE This bird breeds and nests on cliff tops. Over the years it has acquired a number of nicknames including 'The Gooney Bird' to suggest that it is not the most intelligent of our feathered friends.

4 POINT CLUE Species of this bird include black-browed, yellow-nosed, grey-headed, buller's and sooty.

3 POINT CLUE It belongs to the petrel order of birds and some of the species of this marine feeder have been known to have a wing span exceeding 3 metres (12 feet).

2 POINT CLUE This bird was the title of an instrumental No. 1 hit in January 1969.

1 POINT CLUE Legend has it that a sailor will be dogged by bad luck should he kill one of these birds, as it is believed that they are reincarnations of seamen washed overboard.

ANSWER
ALBATROSS

NAME THE COUNTRY

5 POINT CLUE This country is divided into 23 provinces and one federal district, and has a population approaching 35 million. The national anthem of this country is called 'Hear Oh Mortals'.

4 POINT CLUE It is 3,701 kilometres (2,300 miles) in length and one of its main sources of income is oil, a large refinery of which can be found in the town of San Lorenzo.

3 POINT CLUE A golden sun is depicted in the centre of this county's flag and until the 19th century this country was ruled by Spain.

2 POINT CLUE This country's International Rugby Union team is nicknamed the Pumas, however its football team has met with far greater success winning the World Cup on several occasions.

1 POINT CLUE Its capital city is Buenos Aires and in 1982 it went to war with Britain over the Falkland Islands.

ANSWER
ARGENTINA

NAME THE YEAR

5 POINT CLUE This year saw the debut of *My Fair Lady* at Drury Lane and the country of India decided to go metric in this year.

4 POINT CLUE Mike Todd, husband of Elizabeth Taylor, was killed in a plane crash, and Gerald Durrell, the author of *My Family And Other Animals* opened his own zoo on the island of Jersey.

3 POINT CLUE In the movie world Kirk Douglas starred in *The Vikings*, whilst on TV *Blue Peter* made its British television debut.

2 POINT CLUE Columbia Records signed a recording deal with a 17-year-old Cliff Richard. On the other side of the Atlantic Elvis Presley became army private 53310761.

1 POINT CLUE Brazil, with the help of a teenage Pele, won the World Cup, and earlier in the year the football world was in mourning following the decimation of the Busby Babes in the Munich air crash.

ANSWER
1958

NAME THE POP GROUP

5 POINT CLUE This group was formed in 1975 and spent the following year touring London underground clubs supporting the likes of the Clash and the Buzzcocks.

4 POINT CLUE They split up in 1980 following the release of the album *Flogging A Dead Horse* which featured a cover version of the Monkees, hit 'I'm Not Your Stepping Stone'.

3 POINT CLUE In 1979 they appeared in a film called *The Great Rock And Roll Swindle* in which Ronnie Biggs made a cameo appearance. In the same year one of their members died of a drug overdose.

2 POINT CLUE Hit singles include 'C'Mon Everybody', 'Holidays In The Sun' and 'Silly Thing' and they were managed by Malcolm McClaren.

1 POINT CLUE This highly controversial punk rock band was comprised of Johnny Rotten, Steve Jones, Sid Vicious and Paul Cook.

ANSWER
THE SEX PISTOLS

NAME THE TV PROGRAMME

5 POINT CLUE Between 1974 and 1984, 255 episodes were made of this TV show which spawned several spin-offs and was set in the state of Milwaukee.

4 POINT CLUE Actors and actresses who have appeared in this show include Marion Ross, Erin Moran, Danny Most, Anson Williams and Suzie Quatro who was type-cast as a leather-wearing pop singer called Pinky Tuscadero.

3 POINT CLUE This programme was inspired by the success of the film *American Graffiti*, and the cast frequented a burger bar called Arnold's.

2 POINT CLUE Characters in the show included Ralph Malph, Potsy Weber, the Hooper Triplets and the Cunningham family.

1 POINT CLUE The undoubted star of the show was Henry Winkler who played the ultra-cool character of the Fonz.

ANSWER
HAPPY DAYS

NAME THE NOVEL

5 POINT CLUE This classic novel was first published in 1869 and told of savage deeds which were carried out in the depths of Bagworthy Forest.

4 POINT CLUE As a youth the male hero of the novel attended Tiverton Grammar School in the county of Devon.

3 POINT CLUE Chapters in this novel include 'Master Huckaback Comes In', 'Jeremy In Danger', 'John Fry's Errand' and 'Squire Faggus Makes Some Lucky Hits'.

2 POINT CLUE The hero of the novel is called John Ridd and he was played on film in 1951 by the actor Richard Greene.

1 POINT CLUE This famous novel is sub-titled '*A Romance In Exmoor*' and was written by RD Blackmore.

ANSWER
LORNA DOONE

NAME THE COUNTRY

5 POINT CLUE This country is 582 kilometres (362 miles) in length from north to south and averages 188 kilometres (117 miles) in breadth from east to west. The spoken language is one of the Romance languages with spatterings of Arabic and other idioms.

4 POINT CLUE From the 12th century until 1910 this country was a monarchy but in 1910 an armed rising drove King Manuel II into exile and a republic was set up.

3 POINT CLUE The Azores, a group of nine islands, belong to this country and its flag is red and green.

2 POINT CLUE This country occupies the western part of the Iberian peninsula, and is a popular holiday destination especially in the Algarve region.

1 POINT CLUE You would spend Escudos in this country's capital city of Lisbon.

NAME THE FILM

5 POINT CLUE This film won seven Oscars including the Best Film Oscar. A TV series called *Switch* starring Robert Wagner was based on the film and was made shortly after it's Oscar successes.

4 POINT CLUE The film was set in the city of Chicago and a sequel made in 1983 starring Mac Davis and Jackie Gleason bombed at the box office.

3 POINT CLUE The original film was divided into six sections, two of which were called 'The Set Up' and 'The Hook'. The actor who played the film's villain went on to star in the film *Jaws* and died in 1978.

2 POINT CLUE The Oscar-winning music was provided by Scott Joplin and the film was released in 1973.

I POINT CLUE This film co-starred Robert Redford and Paul Newman as a pair of loveable conmen.

ANSWER
THE STING

NAME THE MOUNTAIN

5 POINT CLUE This mountain's rock is comprised chiefly of limestone and the various struggles of climbers of this mountain provide 'entertainment' for onlookers with telescopes at the nearby Kleine Scheidegg.

4 POINT CLUE It consists of three main ridges, the west face of which is said to be the easiest to climb and was first conquered in the 1850s. However, the north-east ridge is considered to be one of the world's most difficult climbs and was not successfully scaled until 1938.

3 POINT CLUE This mountain is situated in the Bernese Alps in Switzerland and is 3,970 metres (4342 yards) high.

2 POINT CLUE Because of the many climbers that have been killed attempting to scale its heights this peak has acquired the nickname of 'The meanest mountain on Earth'.

1 POINT CLUE This mountain provided the setting for a film starring Clint Eastwood and George Kennedy called *The -----Sanction*, the blank space being filled by the mountain's name.

ANSWER
THE EIGER

NAME THE YEAR

5 POINT CLUE In this year the New Hebrides changed its name to the Vanuatu Republic and gained its independence from British and French rule. This year also saw the invention of the compact disc by the electronics company Philips.

4 POINT CLUE Sanjay Gandhi was killed in a plane crash in this year, which also saw the sixpence withdrawn from circulation in Britain.

3 POINT CLUE West Ham United won the FA Cup, Evonne Cawley won the Wimbledon Singles title and Larry Holmes defeated Muhammed Ali.

2 POINT CLUE Abba had their final No. 1 hit with the song 'Super Trouper', and Johnny Logan won the Eurovision Song Contest.

1 POINT CLUE The USA withdrew from the Moscow Olympics and John Lennon was killed by a crazed fan.

ANSWER
1980

NAME THE STAGE SHOW

5 POINT CLUE This famous stage musical celebrated its 10th anniversary in May 1991 and over the years has scooped numerous awards including the Ivor Novello Award for Best Musical.

4 POINT CLUE Songs in this show include 'Moments' and 'The Invitation To The Jellicle Ball', and it was based on a book that was first published in 1939.

3 POINT CLUE The opening night of the show was postponed when the star of the show, Judi Dench, suffered a torn achilles tendon. Whilst that was to prove painful for Dame Judi it provided an opportunity for Elaine Paige who took over the role which catapulted her to stardom.

2 POINT CLUE Characters in the show include Griddlebone, Deuteronomy and Mr Mistoffolees.

1 POINT CLUE It was based on a book written by TS Eliot and the most famous song in the show, 'Memory', went on to become a Top 10 single.

ANSWER
CATS

NAME THE COUNTRY

5 POINT CLUE This country celebrates its Independence Day on the 1st of October, and gained its independence as a member of the Commonwealth in 1960.

4 POINT CLUE It is divided into 30 states and a federal capital territory and its population is almost twice that of the UK.

3 POINT CLUE This country enjoys a tropical climate with the rainy season lasting from April to October. During the dry season the cool harmattan wind blows from the desert.

2 POINT CLUE It forms a coastline in the south with the Gulf of Guinea and is bounded on the east by Cameroon. In 1991 Abuja was declared the federal capital of this country.

1 POINT CLUE It is the most highly populated country in Africa and former Premiership footballer John Fashanu was appointed the Minister for Sport for this country.

ANSWER
NIGERIA

NAME THE YEAR

5 POINT CLUE In this year Boeing launched the 777 and Tokyo's underground railway was subjected to a terrorist attack in the form of nerve gas in March of this year.

4 POINT CLUE Jemima Goldsmith married former test cricketer Imran Khan and Michael Foale became the first British astronaut to walk in space.

3 POINT CLUE Michael Jackson provided the Christmas No. 1 with 'Earth Song', in a year which also saw the deaths of Peter Cook and Ronnie Kray.

2 POINT CLUE David Trimble became the leader of the Ulster Unionists and Hugh Grant was arrested after being found in a compromising position with a prostitute.

1 POINT CLUE Talk Radio took over Radio One's old radio frequencies and this year saw the collapse of the Barings Bank.

ANSWER
1995

NAME THE POP GROUP

....

5 POINT CLUE This group first began singing together in 1958 and released their latest album in 2001. They made their TV debut singing on a show called *Anything Goes* in 1960.

4 POINT CLUE They are the only pop group to have a No. 1 hit single in the UK in the 1960s, 1970s and the 1980s.

3 POINT CLUE Hit records include 'Run To Me', 'Secret Love' and 'For Whom The Bell Tolls'. They enjoyed five UK No. 1 hit singles in the 20th century, the first of which came in 1967.

2 POINT CLUE They also have written many other hits for artists including 'Chain Reaction' for Diana Ross and 'Woman In Love' for Barbra Streisand.

1 POINT CLUE Their flagging career was revived by the 1970s disco boom which saw them record one of the best-selling albums of all time, a soundtrack for the film *Saturday Night Fever*.

ANSWER
THE BEE GEES

NAME THE TV PROGRAMME

5 POINT CLUE This TV programme was first shown in the UK in 1965 and is set in the year 2063.

4 POINT CLUE The show was repeated in 1991 and 2001 and achieved unprecedented ratings causing membership of its official fan club 'Fanderson' to double.

3 POINT CLUE The series spawned two movie spin-offs in 1966 and 1968, and a 1986 Japanese-made cartoon series. The five main characters in the show were named after the first five American astronauts in space.

2 POINT CLUE The villain of this show was known as 'The Hood', and it was created by Gerry and Sylvia Anderson.

1 POINT CLUE This puppet show told of the adventures of the Tracy brothers who formed the organisation known as International Rescue.

ANSWER
THUNDERBIRDS

NAME THE NOVEL

5 POINT CLUE This novel was set in a village called Tevershall and centred around the activities in a mansion called Wragby Hall.

4 POINT CLUE Some of the novel's characters are Ivy Bolton, Tommy Dukes, Charlie May and Lady Cooper.

3 POINT CLUE It has been filmed on several occasions for both the big screen and the small screen. Stars who have appeared in the various productions include Sylvia Kristel, Danielle Darrieux, Nicholas Clay and Sean Bean.

2 POINT CLUE It was written in 1928 but first became available to the general public in 1960 following a landmark court case in which Penguin Books were prosecuted under the Obscene Publications Act.

I POINT CLUE This was the last novel of DH Lawrence and told of the love affair between a gamekeeper called Oliver Mellors and his lady employer.

ANSWER
LADY CHATTERLEY'S LOVER

NAME THE CITY

5 POINT CLUE This city has a land area of 122 square kilometres (47 square miles), a population approaching three quarters of a million, and achieved city status in the USA in 1850.

4 POINT CLUE At the end of World War II this city was the site of an international conference that drafted the UN Charter.

3 POINT CLUE This city can be found on America's Pacific coast and its stock exchange is the base for the Bank of America, one of the world's largest banks.

2 POINT CLUE It has been the subject of numerous hit records over the years including songs recorded by Scott McKenzie, the Village People, Chris Isaak and the Animals.

1 POINT CLUE The central part of this city, famous for its cable cars, stands on a series of hills and according to the song Tony Bennett left his heart here.

ANSWER
SAN FRANCISCO

NAME THE SOAP OPERA CHARACTER

5 POINT CLUE This British soap opera character was born in Bermondsey in 1942 and as a 15-year-old he set up a television and radio repair shop in his parents' house.

4 POINT CLUE In 1976 he bought No. 5 Coronation Street and went on to become a part-owner of a nightclub called the Graffiti Club.

3 POINT CLUE He has had a string of lovers in *Coronation Street* some of whom include Anne Woodley, Suzie Birchall, Maggie Dunlop, Jackie Ingram and Bet Lynch.

2 POINT CLUE He became the arch-enemy of Ken Barlow following an affair with Ken's wife Deirdre, a situation that was worsened when he married Ken's daughter Susan.

1 POINT CLUE This cockney rogue of the rag trade is played by the actor Johnny Briggs.

ANSWER
MIKE BALDWIN

NAME THE BUILDING

5 POINT CLUE The cornerstone of this famous building was laid three weeks before the economic crisis known as 'Black Friday'. 3,400 workers were involved in the construction of this building 14 of whom were killed in accidents.

4 POINT CLUE It was designed by the architects Shreve, Lamb and Harmon, and was built on the former site of the Waldorf Astoria Hotel, which was demolished and moved to an alternative venue.

3 POINT CLUE 60,000 tonnes of steel were erected, 10 million bricks cemented together, 6,500 windows installed and 4,023 kilometres (2,500 miles) of telephone cable were laid in this building, which measures 410 metres (1,345 feet) from the ground to the flagpole.

2 POINT CLUE This building was inaugurated in 1931 at a total estimated cost of $41 million and when it was officially opened it became the world's tallest building.

1 POINT CLUE The climax of the film *King Kong* took place on top of this building found in the city of New York.

ANSWER
THE EMPIRE STATE BUILDING

NAME THE YEAR

5 POINT CLUE In this year Junko Tabei became the first woman to successfully scale Mount Everest and the self-proclaimed Emperor Bokassa became the leader of the Central African Republic.

4 POINT CLUE Films of the year included *Taxi Driver* and *The Eagle Has Landed* whilst No. 1 hits of this year were 'December 63' by the Four Seasons and 'Combine Harvester' by the Wurzels.

3 POINT CLUE A horse called Rag Trade won the Grand National and Harold Wilson quit 10 Downing Street in this year.

2 POINT CLUE *Rocky* won the Oscar for the Best Film and the Dorchester Hotel in London was bought by two Arab businessmen for £9 million.

1 POINT CLUE A goal from Bobby Stokes won the FA Cup for Southampton and the song 'Save All Your Kisses For Me' won the Eurovision Song Contest for the Brotherhood of Man.

ANSWER
1976

NAME THE MYTHOLOGICAL HERO

5 POINT CLUE This hero from Greek mythology was raised by a centaur called Chiron, and during his life had many lovers including Hypsipyle, the Queen of Lemnos, who bore him two sons called Euneus and Thoas.

4 POINT CLUE He was the eldest son of Aeson, and he should rightfully have been the King of Iolcus in Magnesia.

3 POINT CLUE Medea, the daughter of the King of Colchis, fell in love with our hero after Eros had shot her with one of his arrows. They married and lived in Corinth for 10 years but fell out of love, which resulted in Medea being banished from Corinth.

2 POINT CLUE This Greek hero was played in 1963 by Todd Armstrong in a film which co-starred Honor Blackman as the Greek goddess Hera.

I POINT CLUE He led a band of men called the Argonauts, who went in search of the fabled Golden Fleece.

ANSWER
JASON

NAME THE COUNTRY

5 POINT CLUE This country covers an area of 357,034 square kilometres (137,851 square miles) of which 65% is forest and 9% is lake. This country's main source of income is derived from the timber trade.

4 POINT CLUE In the early 19th century this country was an autonomous Grand Duchy of the Russian Empire.

3 POINT CLUE The capital city of this country is nicknamed 'The daughter of the Baltic', and its flag is white with a blue cross.

2 POINT CLUE This country is situated on the Gulf of Bothnia and its currency unit is the markka.

1 POINT CLUE The capital city of this Scandinavian country is Helsinki.

ANSWER
FINLAND

NAME THE YEAR

5 POINT CLUE This year saw two military coups in Fiji and wealthy entrepreneur Peter de Savary bought Lands End.

4 POINT CLUE In the world of politics David Owen resigned as the leader of the SDP and smoking was banned in government buildings.

3 POINT CLUE In the film world Mel Gibson starred in the first *Lethal Weapon* movie and Robin Williams played a wartime disc jockey in the film *Good Morning Vietnam*

2 POINT CLUE Michael Ryan went on the rampage in Hungerford and Princess Anne became Princess Royal.

I POINT CLUE *The Herald of Free Enterprise* sank and Monday the 19th of October of this year became known as 'Black Monday' in the financial world.

ANSWER
1987

NAME THE DUO

5 POINT CLUE This double act first met in a pub called the Half Moon, Holloway, and originally performed together in a pop group called the Outlaws.

4 POINT CLUE Their first hit record in 1978 was entitled 'Strummin', and one of their best-selling albums was entitled 'Boots, Braces And Blue Suede Shoes'.

3 POINT CLUE Their vocals also featured on four hit records for Tottenham Hotspur Football Club, including 'Ossie's Dream'.

2 POINT CLUE Their real names are David Peacock and Charles Hodge.

I POINT CLUE This cockney singing duo had Top 10 hits with the songs 'Rabbit' and 'Ain't No Pleasing You'.

ANSWER
CHAS AND DAVE

NAME THE TV PROGRAMME

5 POINT CLUE This TV programme, first shown in America in 1984 and in Britain one year later, featured a boat called *The St Vitus Dance*, which one of the main characters lived on.

4 POINT CLUE Over the years the show featured guest appearances by a number of pop stars including Phil Collins, Sheena Easton and Glen Frey.

3 POINT CLUE Characters in the show include Detective Larry Zito, Lieutenant Castillo, Detective Trudy Joplin and an alligator called Elvis.

2 POINT CLUE The show was conceived in response to a single two-word memo sent by NBC boss Brandon Tartijoff which read, 'MTV cops'.

1 POINT CLUE The stars of the show were Don Johnson and Philip Michael Thomas who played Crockett and Tubbs.

ANSWER
MIAMI VICE

79

NAME THE SONG

5 POINT CLUE This song has four words in its title and was composed by Jacques Brel with lyrics by Rod McKuen.

4 POINT CLUE On its first release this song was performed by a Canadian singer who had been previously seen in chart action with his wife Susan in a group called the Poppy Family.

3 POINT CLUE It first hit the No. 1 spot in 1974 and in 1999 this song became the Christmas No. 1 hit in the UK, when it was covered by a boy band.

2 POINT CLUE The song tells the poignant story of a man dying of cancer and contains the line "Goodbye, my friends, it's hard to die".

1 POINT CLUE The two artists who topped the charts with this song are Terry Jacks and Westlife.

ANSWER
'SEASONS IN THE SUN'

NAME THE COUNTRY

5 POINT CLUE Three quarters of this country is covered by mountains, the chief range of which is called the Hindu Kush, and its national anthem is entitled 'Soroud-e-Melli'.

4 POINT CLUE The karakuli sheep is bred in this country, which contains only four universities including the Jalalabad University founded in 1962.

3 POINT CLUE The population is very mixed but the most numerous race is the Pushtuns who form approximately half the population. It is estimated that around 3.5 million of that population fled to Pakistan during a 1979 occupation.

2 POINT CLUE This country is bounded on the west by Iran and on the east by Pakistan and China, and the ancient name of this country was Aryana.

1 POINT CLUE Soviet troops invaded this country in 1979 and its capital city is Kabul.

ANSWER
AFGHANISTAN

NAME THE MUSICAL

....

5 POINT CLUE This film musical was directed and choreographed
by Charles Walters and in 1986 was adapted into a UK stage
production starring Trevor Eve and Natasha Richardson.

4 POINT CLUE In the film version Louis Armstrong plays himself
and the main characters are called Mike Connor, Dexter Haven
and Tracey Lord.

3 POINT CLUE It featured many memorable songs including 'Mind
If I Make Love To You', 'Who Wants To Be A Millionaire' and
'True Love'.

2 POINT CLUE This film was released by the MGM Studios in
1956 and was a musical remake of the 1940 film *The
Philadelphia Story*.

I POINT CLUE The stars of this 1956 film are Frank Sinatra, Bing
Crosby and Grace Kelly.

NAME THE CITY

5 POINT CLUE One of the world's oldest universities can be found in this city. It is called the El Azhar University and was founded in 970 AD and specialises in Islamic Law.

4 POINT CLUE This city was occupied by French troops between 1798 and 1801, and its population of over 6 million makes it the most highly populated capital city in Africa.

3 POINT CLUE In 1981 Anwar Al Sadat was assassinated whilst addressing a rally in this city.

2 POINT CLUE This city is situated on the east bank of the River Nile and the pop group Madness caught a night boat to this city in the title of a song.

1 POINT CLUE This city is the capital of Egypt.

ANSWER
CAIRO

NAME THE YEAR

5 POINT CLUE In this year Geoffrey Fisher retired as the Archbishop of Canterbury and U Thant was appointed Secretary General of the United Nations.

4 POINT CLUE The birth control pill became available on the NHS in this year, which also saw the foundation of the World Wildlife Fund.

3 POINT CLUE In October of this year the satirical magazine *Private Eye* was published for the first time, and five months earlier South Africa became a republic, after leaving the Commonwealth.

2 POINT CLUE Elvis Presley had four No. 1 hits in this year including 'Are You Lonesome Tonight'. Other artists to top the charts included Del Shannon, Helen Shapiro and the Shadows.

1 POINT CLUE Tottenham Hotspur won the FA Cup and Yuri Gagarin became the first man in space.

1961
ANSWER

NAME THE SPORT

5 POINT CLUE All competitions in this sport are made up of two parts which are called figures and routines. Two of the most successful exponents in this event are Carolyn Wilson and Caroline Holmyard.

4 POINT CLUE Positions and figures carried out in this sport include the lobster sculls, the egg-beater kick, the Eiffel Tower and the Catalina reverse.

3 POINT CLUE It made its Olympic debut at the Los Angeles Olympics of 1984, and the events include categories for solo competitors, duets and teams, which consists of four or eight members.

2 POINT CLUE Included in the coaching staff are a choreographer, a musical director and a makeup artist.

1 POINT CLUE This sport has been described as a mixture of gymnastics, swimming and dance.

ANSWER
SYNCHRONISED SWIMMING

NAME THE ISLAND

5 POINT CLUE This island measures 225 kilometres (140 miles) at it's greatest length, and 96 kilometres (60 miles) at its greatest breadth. On average the 1.5 million tourists that visit the island annually outnumber the citizens.

4 POINT CLUE The flag of this island country is the only flag in the world to contain an outline of the country on it.

3 POINT CLUE In 1974 a coup d'etat was launched against President Makarios and he was replaced by Nikos Sampson. Popular holiday destinations on this island include Larnaca and Limassol.

2 POINT CLUE This island is the third largest island in the Mediterranean Sea and is about 64 kilometres (40 miles) from the nearest point of Asia Minor.

1 POINT CLUE From 1925–1960 this island was a Crown Colony and its capital is Nicosia.

ANSWER
CYPRUS

NAME THE YEAR

5 POINT CLUE In this year the volcano Nevado del Ruiz erupted, burying the Colombian town of Armero, and in this year Rupert Murdoch bought a 50% share of the film company Twentieth Century Fox.

4 POINT CLUE Gary Kasparov became the youngest ever Chess Champion and Clive Sinclair launched the C5 tricycle.

3 POINT CLUE There was an explosion aboard the Greenpeace flagship, *The Rainbow Warrior* and Clive Lloyd played in his 110th and final test appearance for the West Indies.

2 POINT CLUE Kevin Moran became the first player to be sent off in an FA Cup Final, whilst snooker fans stayed up until the early hours of the morning to watch TV coverage of Dennis Taylor's dramatic victory over Steve Davis in the final of the World Snooker Championship.

1 POINT CLUE This year saw the disaster of the Bradford City football-ground fire and Wembley Stadium was rocking to the sound of the Live Aid concert.

ANSWER
1985

NAME THE POP GROUP

5 POINT CLUE This pop group was formed in 1991 and performed their first gig at the Boardwalk Club supporting a band called Sweet Jesus.

4 POINT CLUE The driving force behind this group was a former roadie for the Inspiral Carpets, and they made their TV debut in 1994 on the controversial show *The Word*.

3 POINT CLUE They took their name from a Swindon sports centre and their debut album was entitled 'Definitely Maybe'.

2 POINT CLUE Their first single 'Supersonic' reached No. 31 in the charts and their first chart-topping single was entitled 'Some Might Say'.

1 POINT CLUE This Manchester-based group include the warring Gallagher brothers in their line-up.

ANSWER
OASIS

NAME THE TV CHARACTER

5 POINT CLUE This TV character first appeared in a novel called *Last Bus To Woodstock* which was adapted into a radio serial in 1985.

4 POINT CLUE Actors who have appeared in the many TV films made include Richard Briers, Philip Middlemiss, Sean Bean, Brian Cox, Geoffrey Palmer and Sir John Gielgud.

3 POINT CLUE As a university student this character was a member of an organisation known by the acronym SPARTA, which stands for Society for the Promotion of Real Traditional Ale.

2 POINT CLUE He made his TV debut in a feature-length episode called *The Dead Of Jericho*, and his superior officer is called Superintendent Strange, who is played by James Grout.

I POINT CLUE This character played by John Thaw was created by Colin Dexter and it was revealed that his first name is Endeavour.

ANSWER
INSPECTOR MORSE

NAME THE SONG

5 POINT CLUE This famous song was actually written in 1903 by Theodore F Morse and Edward Madden.

4 POINT CLUE This song went on to top the UK singles charts for six weeks on the Columbia Record Label.

3 POINT CLUE The song has three words in its title and in 1980 it was covered by the spoof punk-rock band Splodgenessabounds.

2 POINT CLUE It was the last No.1 hit of the 1960s and it was performed by a famous Australian entertainer.

1 POINT CLUE This song sung by Rolf Harris told the story of a pair of brothers called Joe and Jack.

ANSWER
TWO LITTLE BOYS

NAME THE COUNTRY

5 POINT CLUE The national day of this country falls on December 5th and this country became a constitutional monarchy in 1952.

4 POINT CLUE The capital city of this country can be found at the mouth of the River Chao Phraya. The country is bounded on the west by Myanmar and on the north-east by Laos.

3 POINT CLUE The country's main seaport is called Sattahip and the chief exports leaving this port include rice, rubber and precious stones.

2 POINT CLUE You would spend the Baht in this country and over 90% of its population are Buddhists.

1 POINT CLUE Bangkok is the capital city of this country.

ANSWER
THAILAND

NAME THE FILM

5 POINT CLUE The supporting cast of this 1993 blockbuster movie included Bob Peck, José Mazello, Martin Ferrero and Samuel L Jackson.

4 POINT CLUE This film won Oscars for sound and visual effects and in 1997 a sequel followed. The films proved so popular that they became the theme for a thrill-seeking ride at the Universal Studios in Orlando.

3 POINT CLUE Dr Hammond, Dr Grant and Dr Sattler are three of the main characters in this film.

2 POINT CLUE The film was directed by Stephen Spielberg and was based on a novel by Michael Crichton.

1 POINT CLUE The 1993 original featured a memorable car chase in which a jeep was pursued by a tyrannosaurus rex.

ANSWER
JURASSIC PARK

NAME THE COUNTY

5 POINT CLUE This English county took its name from its tidal waters and contains the towns of Swanage and Bridport.

4 POINT CLUE It is noted for its picturesque beaches including Chesil Beach and Lulworth Cove. Famous buildings in this county include Sherborne Abbey and Corfe Castle.

3 POINT CLUE One can visit the town of Cerne Abbas which features on its hillside a famous chalk-outlined man, 55 metres (180 feet) tall known as the Cerne Abbas Giant.

2 POINT CLUE The Tolpuddle Martyrs hailed from this county, and Thomas Hardy was born here in the town of Higher Bockhampton.

1 POINT CLUE This small county measures only 96 by 64 kilometres (60 by 40 miles) and forms borders with several other counties including Hampshire.

ANSWER
DORSET

NAME THE YEAR

5 POINT CLUE In this year Prince Charles attended the funeral of King Olaf of Norway, and the Press Complaints Commission replaced the Press Council.

4 POINT CLUE The high street banks introduced TESSA accounts and the Warsaw Pact was dissolved.

3 POINT CLUE Michael Watson almost died after fighting Chris Eubank, and Prince William underwent an operation on his skull after being accidentally hit with a golf club.

2 POINT CLUE John McCarthy was released by Lebanese terrorists, and Brian Adams topped the charts throughout the summer of this year with the theme from *Robin Hood, Prince Of Thieves*.

1 POINT CLUE Major supermarkets began opening on Sunday and Operation Desert Storm was launched to eject the Iraqi Army from Kuwait.

1991
ANSWER

NAME THE SPORT

5 POINT CLUE The earliest record of this sport dates back to 23 BC, and until 1919 female spectators were banned. The first professional club for this sport was established in 1751.

4 POINT CLUE As a youngster in order to enter this association you must weigh a minimum of 75 kilos (165 pounds), stand at least 173 cm (68 inches) tall and have the permission of a parent or guardian.

3 POINT CLUE Exercises carried out by the participants include the matawari splits and shiko stomping, whilst a coach is known as an oyakata.

2 POINT CLUE The headquarters of this sports association can be found at Ryogoku, and the centre of a stadium is called a dohyo.

1 POINT CLUE This is the national sport of Japan and a Grand Champion in this sport attains the title of Yokozuna.

ANSWER
SUMO WRESTLING